Scary Stories
The Scarier the Better?

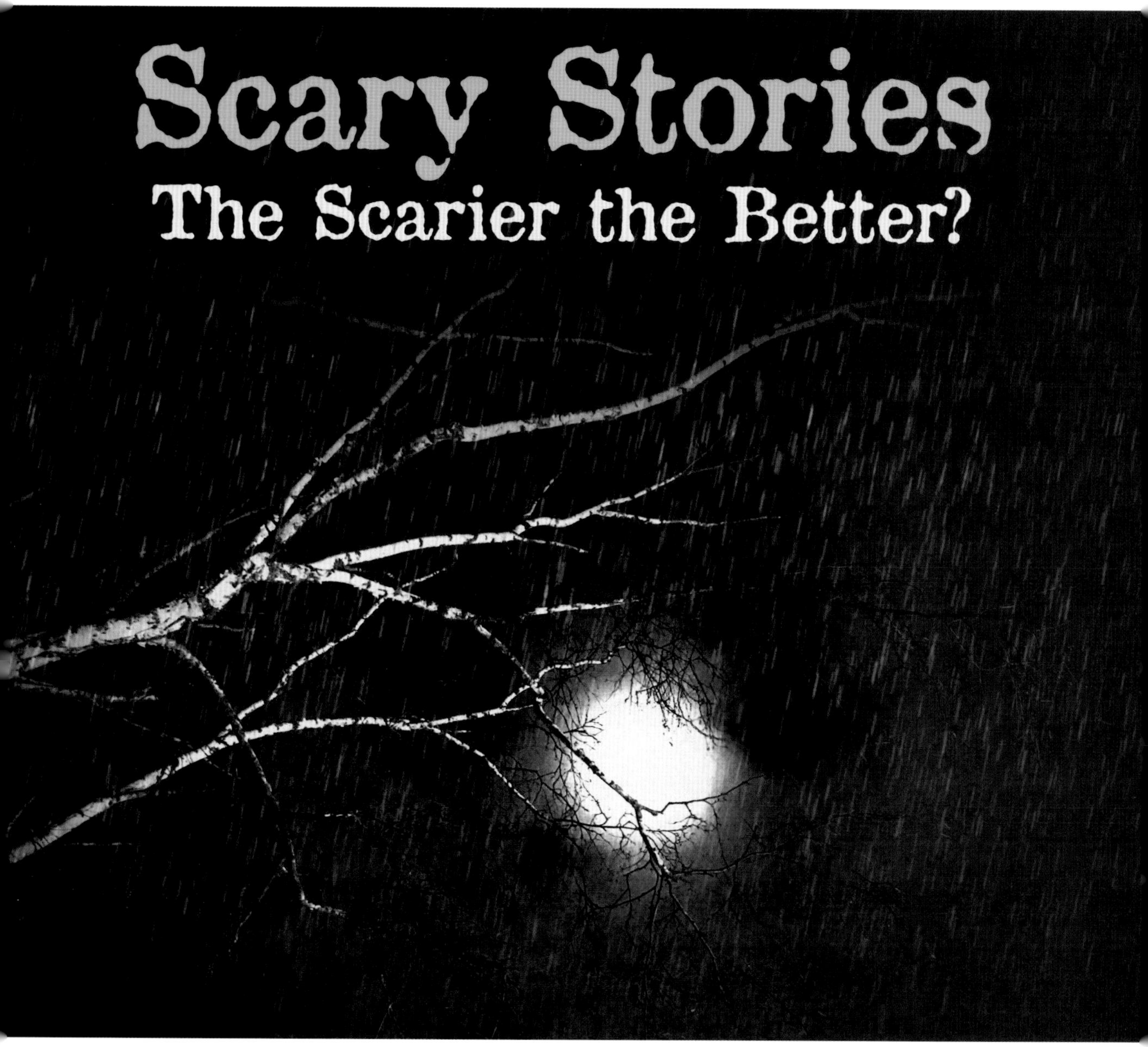

Series Consultant: Linda Hoyt

Flying Start
to Literacy®

T0359879

Contents

Introduction

Scary stories – why do we tell them?

Many people listen to scary stories "just for the fun of it." They enjoy the feeling of being scared!

What makes a story a scary story differs from person to person. What scares me might not scare you . . . and what scares you might not scare me!

Do you like scary stories? And if so, do you say: The scarier the better?

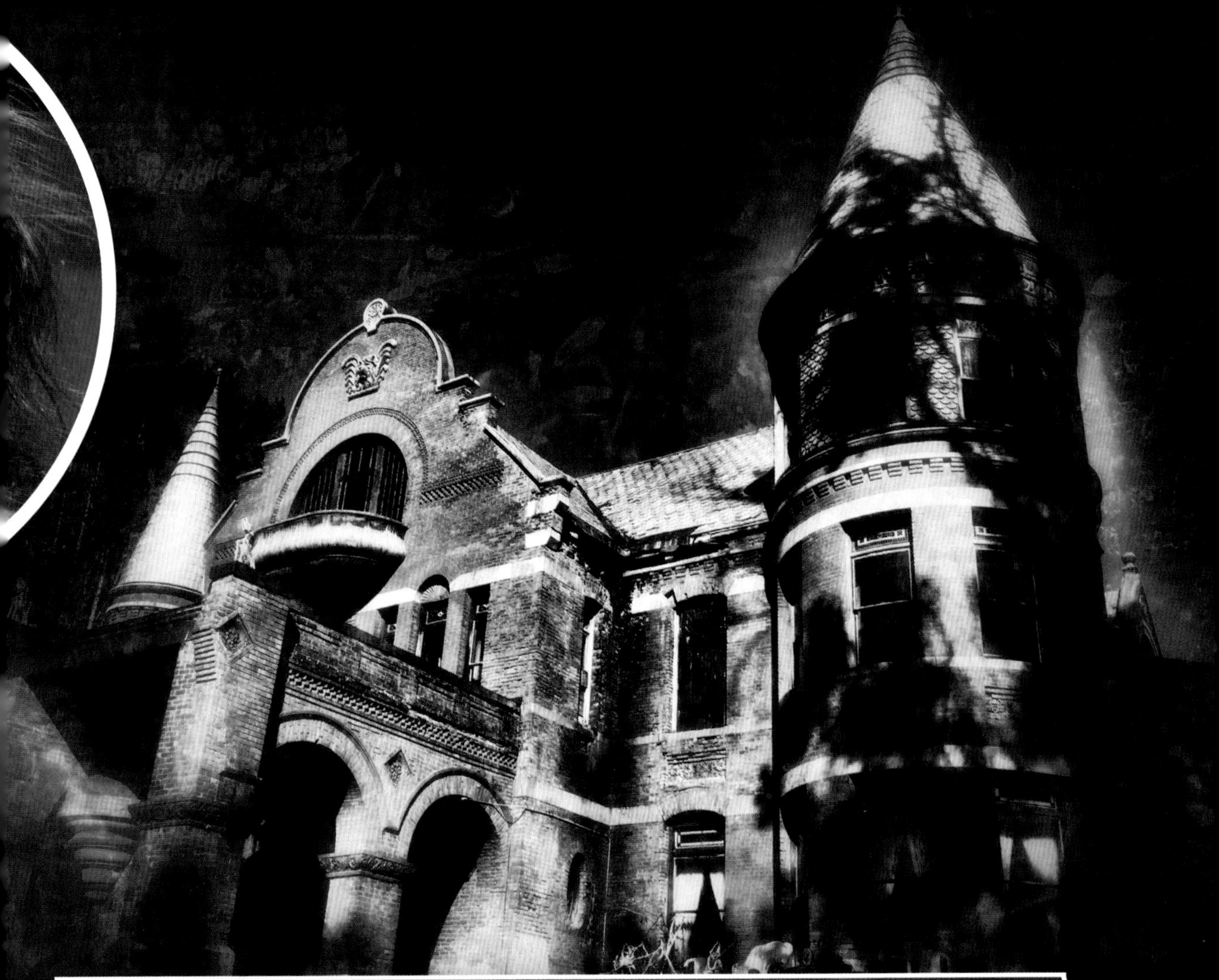

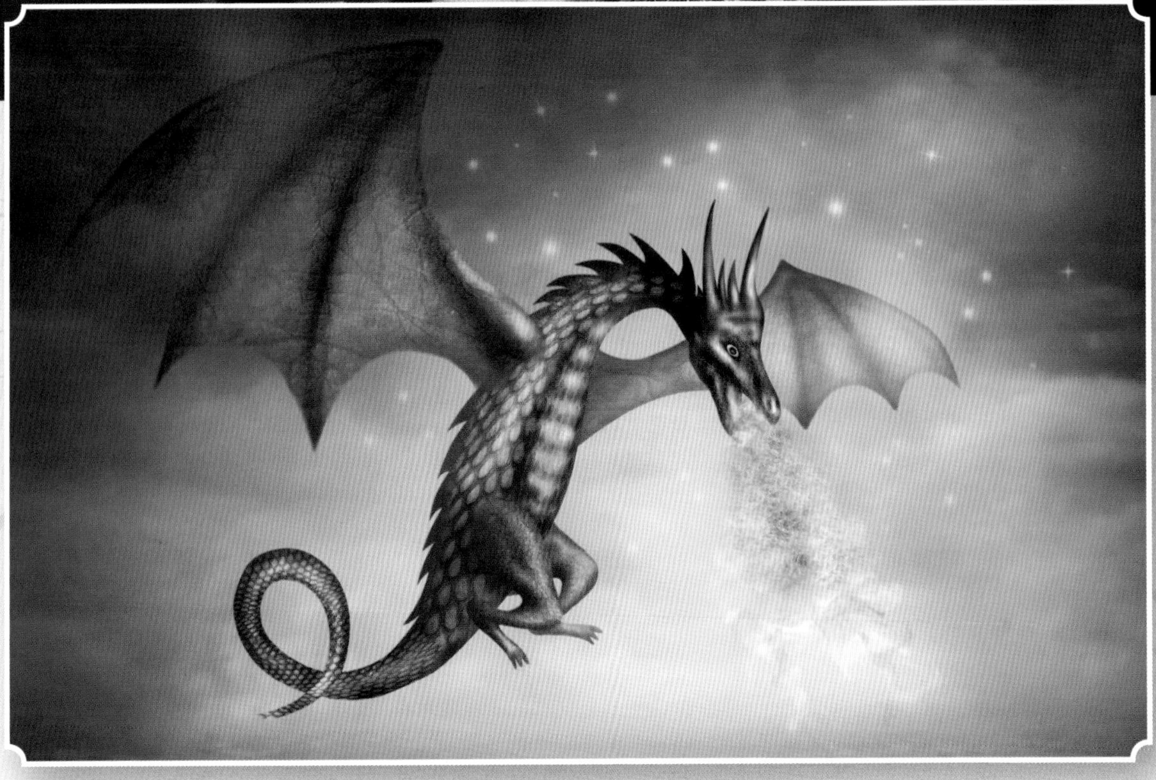

Scary characters

All good scary stories need someone or something to scare us.

What is the scariest character you have ever read about? Why were you scared?

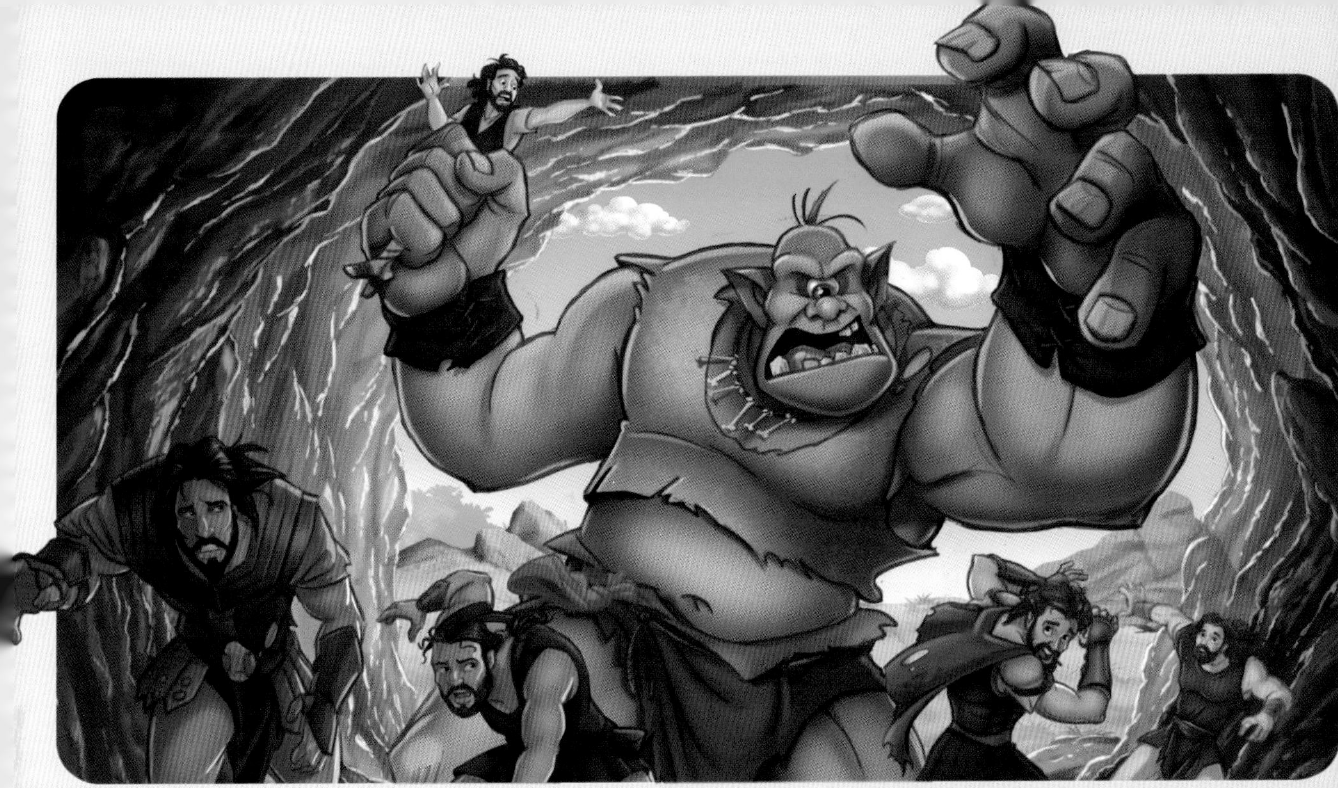

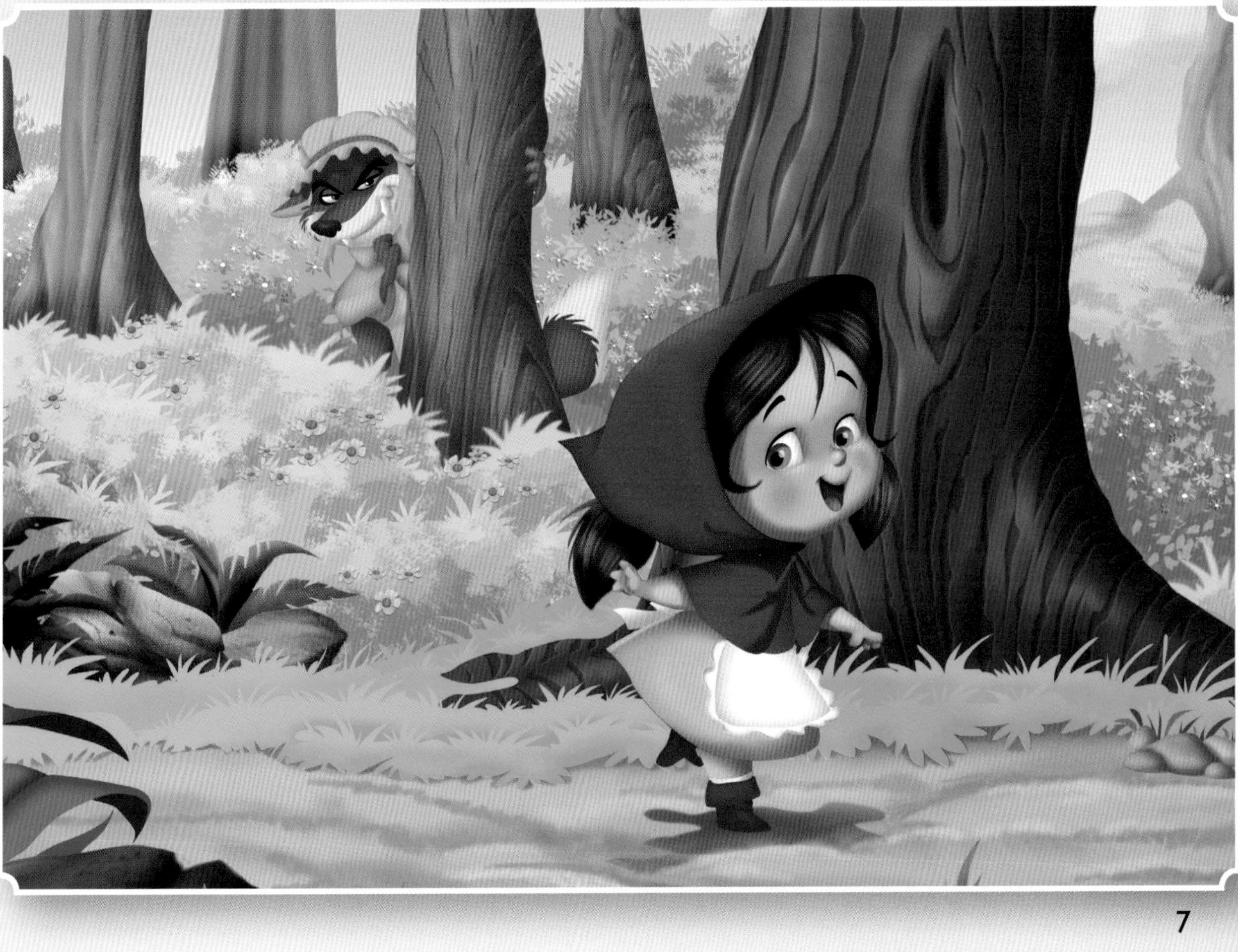

Speak out!

Read what these students think about scary stories.

Why do some people like to be scared? What scary stories do you like?

I usually like scary stories, but it all depends. It's okay for a story to be scary in a book that doesn't have pictures. But if I watch a movie or a TV program, the images stay in my head – that can be really scary.

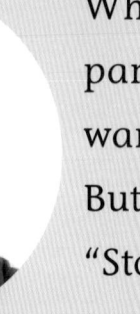

When I listen to or watch scary stories, part of me gets really curious, and I want to keep listening or watching. But another part of me says, "Stop! Stop!"

 I'm okay with scary stories that are fantasy. But real scary stories are terrifying – stories about people who are trapped in buildings after an earthquake, that's scary!

 I don't understand why people want to get scared. Just close the book or switch off the TV – you're the one in control.

Don't tell scary stories

Written by Nathan Gillespie

Nathan's mum and dad saw a scary movie, and they told their children, Nathan and David, about it. Nathan was okay, but David had nightmares.

Should young children be told scary stories? What do you think?

Last night, my brother came into my room shivering with fear.

"What's wrong?" I asked David.

"I had a bad dream about the movie. I dreamed that monsters invaded our city."

"It's okay, David. It was just a dream. Monsters aren't real and can't hurt you."

"But it is still scary to think about it happening," said David.

"Don't worry about it. I'll take you back to bed."

The next morning, I told Mum and Dad about David being scared. They said not to worry – and that David would be fine that night.

But the same thing happened at bedtime.

"Bad dream again?" I asked.

"Yeah," said David.

"What happened?"

"The monsters came to our apartment building, and they grabbed Dad and took him away."

I took David back to his room and stayed until he went to sleep.

The next morning, I had dark rings under my eyes.

"You look like one of the monsters from the film," said Dad.

"David woke me up again," I said.

"Oh," said Dad, looking a little worried.

"We need to find a way to make David realise monsters aren't real and can't hurt him," I said.

"I know just the way to do it," said Dad.

"How?"

"When I was a little boy, I was really scared of vampires. One day, my dad showed me a drawing of a vampire, and it made me realise that vampires weren't that scary. I had just made them a big thing in my head."

"Okay, I guess we may as well try it."

That afternoon, when David got home from school, Dad took him into his office.

"I know that ever since I told you about the movie, you've been scared of monsters. I know you may think this is a bad idea, but let's try watching some of the movie."

"Okay," said David in a shaky voice.

As I watched David's face, I could see he was completely terrified. But after watching the movie for five minutes, he looked pretty relaxed.

"The monsters aren't actually that scary," he said.

The next morning, when I went downstairs, David was eating breakfast.

"Did you have any bad dreams last night?" I asked.

"Yeah, I had one, but I was able to calm myself down enough to go back to sleep."

"That's great! It felt good to get a whole night's rest without you waking me up," I joked.

Writing scary stories

Many of us like reading or listening to scary stories. But, what about writing one? Author Kerrie Shanahan shares some of her writing secrets for spooky stories.

What sort of scary story would you like to write?

Q. Kerrie, how do you get ideas for your scary stories?

A. I think about what scares people – the dark, being lost, spiders and fictional creatures such as dragons. I use these "scary" things as a starting point for ideas.

Q. What is the key to making readers really scared?

A. It is the "not knowing" that is often the scariest part. I build the suspense. I want readers to be on the edge of their seats thinking: *Oh no! What's going to happen?*

Q. What are your top tips for writing a terrifying tale?

A. Make the hero of your story likeable and real. Then, when this character is petrified, the reader will be, too! Set your story in a spooky, eerie place, and describe the atmosphere – what does it sound like, feel like, look like?

And there needs to be a surprise – something that suddenly shocks your readers and scares their socks off!

How to write about your opinion

State your opinion

Think about the main question in the introduction on page 4 of this book. What is your opinion?

Research

Look for other information that you need to back up your opinion.

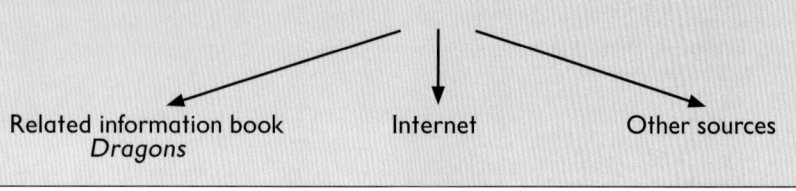

| Related information book *Dragons* | Internet | Other sources |

Make a plan

Introduction

How will you "hook" the reader to get them interested?

Write a sentence that makes your opinion clear.

List reasons to support your opinion.

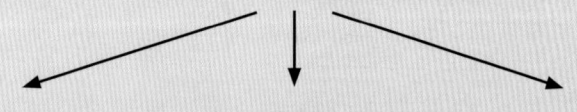

| Support your reason with examples. | Support your reason with examples. | Support your reason with examples. |

Conclusion

Write a sentence that makes your opinion clear. Leave your reader with a strong message.

Publish

Publish your writing.

Include some graphics or visual images.